FLOWERS
for ALL

FLOWERS
for ALL

MODERN FLORAL ARRANGEMENTS FOR
BEAUTY, JOY, AND MINDFULNESS EVERY DAY

SUSAN MCLEARY
photographs by EE Berger

CHRONICLE BOOKS
SAN FRANCISCO

To Chaad, Leda, and Maceo.

It's not too late to turn you into flower people.

Love, Mom

Library of Congress Cataloging-in-Publication Data

Names: McLeary, Susan, author. | Berger, E. E., photographer.

Title: Flowers for all : modern floral arrangements for beauty, joy, and mindfulness every day / Susan McLeary; photographs by E.E. Berger.

Description: San Francisco : Chronicle Books, [2023]

Identifiers: LCCN 2022037938 | ISBN 9781797215662 (hardcover)

Subjects: LCSH: Flower arrangement.

Classification: LCC SB449 .M387 2023 | DDC 745.92--dc23/eng/20220822

LC record available at https://lccn.loc.gov/2022037938

Manufactured in China.

Design by Rachel Harrell.
Photographs by EE Berger.

10 9 8 7 6 5 4 3 2

Chronicle books and gifts are available at special quantity discounts to corporations, professional associations, literacy programs, and other organizations. For details and discount information, please contact our premiums department at corporatesales@chroniclebooks.com or at 1-800-759-0190.

Chronicle Books LLC
680 Second Street
San Francisco, California 94107
www.chroniclebooks.com

CONTENTS

INTRODUCTION

Flowers Are for All 8

BEFORE FLOWERING 15

FINDING FLOWERS AND
BRINGING THEM HOME

- Tools and Techniques
  for Creating Your
  Arrangements 17

- Caring for Your
  Cut Flowers 20

DISPLAYING FLOWERS

- Vases and Vessels 24

- Simple Design Mechanics
  and Techniques 29

- Setting the Scene 35

- Wiring 36

FLOWERS FOR ME 39

Flower Yourself 40

Floral Support 45

Floral Meditation 48

Art Muse 53

Reflecting Pool 56

Petite Armature 61

Aromatherapy 64

Color Study 69

Studio Scene 72

Floral Gallery 77

FLOWERS FOR FRIENDS 81

Perennial Present 82

Simply Strung 87

Trumpet Beads 90

Artful Offering 95

Avocado Inspiration 98

Summer Still Life 103

Dahlia Drama 106

Wreath Party 111

Celebratory Spiral 114

Fall Fruits 119

FLOWERS FOR ALL 123

Bloom Room 124

Garden Variety 129

Spring Scene 132

Complementary Tablescape 137

Petal Play 140

Garden Gathering 145

Flower Shower 148

Wall Flowers 153

Aerial Amaryllis 156

Flower Tower 160

Reliables 164

Resources 169

Acknowledgments 172

FLOWERS ARE FOR ALL

I fell in love with the medium of flowers entirely by chance. About two decades ago, a friend asked me to arrange the flowers for her wedding. I said yes to the challenge, trusting my creative leanings would respond to the task, but I honestly didn't have any particular feelings about the work ahead. I can distinctly remember the exact moment I realized that I'd found something very special: I was alone, standing in my kitchen in the middle of the night, ankle-deep in detritus, surrounded by buckets and buckets of flowers, with a considerable amount of work left to do. I realized with a start that I hadn't stopped to eat, drink, or rest in several hours. I was so completely absorbed in the work that everything else had melted away. I also sensed that the sappy little smile on my face had been there the entire time. It was an intoxicating and novel mix of seemingly discordant emotions—serenity, excitement, joy, exhaustion, and total engagement.

I'd never felt so completely transfixed by a task before. I recognized

that when you find an activity that makes you feel this way, you owe it to yourself to explore it fully. From that moment on, I became completely obsessed with being a florist.

Looking back, I see that floral design is the perfect creative expression for me, as it weaves together my lifelong fascination with nature and my love of fashion design, accessory design, and art. I'm so grateful I found a practice that has brought so much richness and enjoyment to my life. Years later, now a floral design instructor and writer, I am most interested in welcoming everyone—not just florists—to engage with flowers. Over the years, I've benefited tremendously from how they've captured my imagination and calmed my mind. I hope to pass on the lessons they have offered me over the years.

While I am a florist, this isn't meant to be a traditional floral design book. You won't find detailed step-by-step instruc-

tions or principles of design here. Floral design is a visual art form, and like any other, it possesses rich design principles to explore, but the ideas within this book are kept intentionally simple and approachable to inspire everyone to participate in this gratifying practice. This is a book meant to invite you to simply engage with flowers more often. It's meant to encourage us all to see flowers and natural materials as accessible art supplies to be used to enrich our lives and enliven living spaces. Flowers continuously inspire me, delight me, pique my curiosity, give me pause, and add to my daily well-being. I hope that my ideas invite you to connect with flowers too.

Nearly all of the materials I've used in this book are seasonal and locally sourced. I wanted to create with materials available to me at any given time instead of exotics available only to those of us with access to professional floral wholesalers or specialty sources. I hope this makes the projects here feel accessible to as many people as possible. I gathered the bulk of my materials from my (very) humble garden and yard, my neighborhood (with permission), and my local farmers' market, grocers, and flower farms. By deliberately valuing what is available locally, we nurture a pride of place that not only benefits us personally but also boosts the local economy, supports local growers, and reduces environmental harm. Locally sourced materials also convey a sense of season, making them that much more evocative and meaningful. Over the years, this deliberate practice has strengthened my appreciation for the place in the world and time that I inhabit.

Some of the flowers in this book may seem ordinary—that was also intentional. Even the ubiquitous patio geranium is beautiful, smells delightful, and offers nostalgia and vibrant color. I deliberately practice the act of seeing beauty in what is available to me at any given time. I encourage you to find inspiration in familiar everyday plants. When displayed thoughtfully, they can capture our attention and appear novel once more. As the seasons change, pay attention to what is available to you in the green spaces you have access to. The ever-changing, ephemeral nature of flowers has much to teach us about living in the present and relishing the moment. I hope to inspire you to regularly pause to observe the natural world and invite flowers into your home often. I hope they offer you the same sense of serene engagement they have offered me.

I've organized this book into four sections. We begin with Before Flowering (the basics), followed by projects in these sections: Flowers for Me, Flowers for Friends, and Flowers for All. There are thirty ideas on how you might create with flowers—for yourself, for friends and loved ones, and for small gatherings. Living with flowers can remind us that:

- Art is for all.
- We are all creative.
- Flowers and plants are accessible to all.
- Nature is endlessly inspiring.
- Locality and seasonality matter.
- Flowers have mood-boosting qualities.
- Pausing and appreciating moments of beauty regularly enhances well-being.
- The practice of floral appreciation has value.
- The value of flowers is not tied to their longevity.

In Flowers for Me, you'll find my favorite ways to display flowers in my home, just for me. I buy and grow flowers for myself for many reasons. They lift my mood, they spark creativity, they remind me of the past, they create pause, they calm my busy mind, and they simply make my daily life more colorful and beautiful. Just as you might gather seasonal ingredients and cook a nourishing meal for yourself, gathering flowers and creating for your own pleasure is an act of self-care. I invite you to treat yourself to this simple beautifying practice.

In Flowers for Friends, you'll find ideas for creating simple floral gifts or intimate displays for friends and loved ones. I've always recognized that flowers make a perfect gift, even before I was a florist. Flowers are emotive and evocative—I've never seen a person receive them without pausing to smell them, touch them, or otherwise relish them. They make meaningful gifts that envelop the senses of those lucky enough to receive them. I also consider displays created for guests as gifts of sorts. Guests may not always leave with these pieces in tow, but they can feel that the displays were created for them, and that in itself is a gesture that lifts the spirits and elevates any gathering.

In Flowers for All, there are ideas on how to use flowers and natural materials to create celebratory settings—perfect for marking the important moments of our lives. Engaging centerpieces, floral installations, and large-scale floral displays should not be limited to professional florists. I hope you enjoy my approachable yet impactful ideas to create inspiring floral spaces for yourself.

The Reliables and Resources sections provides more information and links to the many vendors noted throughout the three main sections.

BEFORE FLOWERING

FINDING FLOWERS AND BRINGING THEM HOME

One of the questions I receive most is "Where do you get your flowers?" Because I am a florist, I have year-round access to a dizzying array of flowers from around the globe. I am often tempted by these enticing treasures, but I find the most satisfaction in sourcing materials from my own special place on the map. I am based in Michigan (USDA gardening zone 5), so I have to work a little harder to be able to design flowers year-round. Our growing season is only about six months long—a limitation that has forced me to think creatively in the cold months and appreciate the warm ones that much more. I like to approach sourcing by starting in my own backyard and working outward from there. Even a humble home garden like mine can provide plenty of inspiring materials. I've built my garden over time, adding continually bit by bit, choosing materials that lend themselves to home arranging. At the moment, I am growing blooming shrubs including lilac, hydrangea, deutzia, spirea, and ninebark; foliage such as mint, artemisia, heuchera, and brunnera; flowers like hellebore, peonies, and iris; and vines such as clematis, hops, raspberry, and luffa gourd. My garden is small and seasonal, so I can't depend solely on home-grown materials, but it is wonderful to be able to open the back door and browse around for a bit of this or that to fill out an arrangement. Beyond my own garden, I look for other spaces that I have access to: the wild brambles at the edge of our property, my neighbor's overgrown forsythia hedge, the honey locust pods that fall and litter the street near my house, the abundant hellebore patch at my mom's, my friend's cherry trees, or the plentiful vine that hangs over and blocks the pedestrian path near my neighborhood swim club.

It goes without saying that one must always ask permission before gathering or trimming on someone else's property. I'm always a bit timid when approaching people with this ask, but I've found over the years that people almost always say yes. They don't mind my urban foraging behaviors because my careful trimming makes use of materials that would otherwise become overgrown and unruly. They would eventually need to be trimmed and discarded anyway, so why not allow an enthusiastic volunteer to do the work instead?

Beyond my own yard and the urban foraging spaces I have access to are the true gems—the local flower and vegetable farms, nurseries, and greenhouses that supply the community. These treasured sources provide most of my materials. I cannot overstate my immense appreciation for their commitment and passion for growing. Local flowers, produce, and plants are fresher, healthier, more interesting, and just plain better than anything shipped in from afar. I urge you to connect with and support the local growers in your area. Online directories such as Local Harvest and the National Farmers Market Directory (NFMD) will help you find local farmers' markets, and resources such as the Association of Specialty Cut Flower Growers' Local

Flowers directory and the Slow Flowers searchable database (see Resources, page 169) will help you connect with flower growers and sellers in your area. When the killing frost arrives, and the Michigan growing season comes to a close, I widen my circle and source materials from farmers in warmer states, local greenhouses, flower wholesalers, and even local grocery stores.

Locally grown materials do shine with a special energy, but floral appreciation can be a year-round practice, no matter your locale.

TOOLS and TECHNIQUES for CREATING YOUR ARRANGEMENTS

The tool chest in my home studio is overstuffed with floral knives, clippers, shears, scissors, pliers, and all manner of implements that I've collected over the years, but you don't need such an arsenal to be able to arrange flowers daily. The tools I reach for most often are my pruning shears, slim-tipped snips, and a floral knife.

The shears are used to harvest and trim branches and thick or woody stems. Bypass shears— the type with two strong blades that pass each other as they cut—are the best type to choose for this work. They can handle dense branch material easily, and they also cut cleanly, preserving the cellular structure of the stem as they pass through instead of squeezing or crushing it like the anvil type. This is important, as the plant uses the tubular cells in the stem to hydrate the foliage and flowers. Crushing obstructs the upward intake of water by destroying these straw-like cells. Also, as they are crushed, they release their contents into the water in the vase, clouding it and promoting bacterial growth that can shorten the vase life of the arrangement.

Slim-tipped snips are used to harvest and trim delicate herbaceous stems and to edit out extraneous or damaged foliage or lateral shoots from stems. The narrow tip reaches easily into the specific area you want to snip without damaging the surrounding structures.

You can successfully design just about anything with just shears and snips at the ready, but over the years my floral knife has become my favorite, most essential tool. It may be because the straight blade looks a little dangerous, requires a bit of mastery, and has a sort of cool factor—a bit like learning to drive a standard transmission instead of an automatic. This is the tool I reach for in my daily designing, the one I can't travel without.

To use a floral knife properly, hold it firmly in your dominant hand with the stem between the bases of your index finger and your thumb, and position your thumb parallel to the blade of the knife, in a thumb's-up position. Keep your knife hand rigid and your thumb away from the blade at all times. Use your nondominant hand to introduce stems to the cutting hand. To cut, place each stem, one at a time, into the crook between your thumb and the knife blade. The end of the stem will extend past the back of your hand. Use your thumb to secure the stem below where you want to make the cut, holding it in place within the crook of your palm. You can either use your nondominant hand to pull the stem up and through the blade or use your dominant hand to pull the knife through the stem while your nondominant hand holds the stem still. (There are helpful videos online on how to use a flower knife—a picture is worth a thousand words! Once you view and try out the options, you'll soon learn which is most comfortable for you.) Always make sure your knife is clean and sharp, and be sure to cut each stem on an angle. This ensures that when the flowers are placed in a vase, the cut end of the stem won't rest flush with the bottom, potentially blocking it and preventing the uptake of water.

CARING *for* YOUR CUT FLOWERS

The challenge for a florist is to create perfectly timed art out of natural, fleeting elements. Just as a chef would, we carefully select and gather our ingredients, coax them to perfection, arrange them thoughtfully, and "serve" them to our happy recipients.

Professional florists can choose from many processes and products that boost freshness and maximize the life span of fresh flowers. But what do we really need, to care for our flowers? I'm a foodie as well as a florist, and I like to explore the parallels between the food and floral worlds.

Consider for a moment the mass-produced grocery shelf loaf of bread. Check that ingredients list. It is not made simply of flour, yeast, and water; it's full of stabilizers, preservatives, and other questionable ingredients, all added to increase the shelf life of the loaf and guarantee "value" to the customer. Similarly, floral foods, holding solutions, and hydrating solutions increase the vase life of flowers, making them more valuable to the recipient. But do we really need our bread or our flowers to last an unnatural two weeks? At what cost? While I do appreciate the importance of some of these products and methods, especially for the growers who must deliver flowers in a condition that promises further life in an arrangement, I purposely keep my own flower care practices straightforward, natural, and simple.

This starts with harvesting. When I gather from my home garden or neighborhood sources, or cut from a flower farm, I go early in the morning, when the air is still cool and the plants are plump with stored water. If morning gathering isn't possible, I harvest in the evening, when the plants are well fed—full of carbohydrate from the photosynthetic activities of the day. As I gather, each stem goes into a clean bucket of fresh water as soon as possible. These simple, gentle practices reduce the chance that the stems will become stressed or compromised during harvest. When I return home, I flush the buckets and fill them once more with fresh, clean water and lay my bounty on my worktable. I trim off extraneous or damaged foliage, as well as any greenery that may fall below the waterline. I also rinse off especially dirty materials at this time. Longevity in the arrangement depends largely on limiting the bacterial growth in the water source, so it really does pay to meticulously clean your materials and remove any dirt or plant matter that could find its way into the water source. After cleaning and trimming, setting up materials to perform well depends on the conditions of the environment they are kept in. After flowers and foliage that would lie below the waterline are removed from the plant, the remaining contributors to wilt are tempera-

ture, relative humidity, chilling drafts, and direct sunlight. Flowers are most robust when stored in a cool, dark, slightly humid place before display, and displayed away from heat registers, fans, air conditioners, or intense direct sunlight. Be sure to freshen vases often, ideally dumping out the old water, rinsing, and replacing with fresh water at least every other day, and giving stems a fresh cut.

Flowers that will be arranged in a water-filled vessel will have what they need to be displayed for their life span, but what about the wearable pieces on page 88 and 92 or aerial displays such as the Flower Shower on page 148? These celebratory short-term floral displays have special considerations. When making wearable floral pieces—corsages, crowns, boutonnieres, and floral jewelry—we typically remove the stems completely, so stem wilt is not a concern. The concern is hydrating the surface of the petals and leaves to keep them looking their best for the amount of time they'll be worn. For a typical event, I estimate this to be about eight hours. To create these pieces, I rely on long-lasting materials that I know will perform well (aptly called "reliables"; see page 164), but I also use more delicate materials and prepare them to perform longer by spraying them with water, covering them with damp paper towels (or similar), and tucking them into a simple airtight container. This "hydration chamber" process isn't a new one—florists have been boosting materials this way for years. I was lucky enough to study with legendary floral artists Hitomi Gilliam and Gregor Lersch, and I learned this simple yet transformative process from them.

There is nothing fancy about these chambers—washed plastic food containers, resealable airtight plastic bags, or lidded storage bins all work well. Line the container with paper towels, spray them with water, lay in your materials, spray them with water, and "tuck them in" with a top layer of damp paper towels. Spray the underside of the lid and the walls of the chamber with a fine mist of water for good measure, and store in a cool place. As the materials rest in the chamber, the water vapor inside is forced into the pores on the surface of the petals, stems, and leaves. The paper towel adds to the effect, but also prevents too much water from pooling under the flowers and (I hypothesize) protects them from tissue damage. The materials emerge from the chamber plump and completely hydrated from the outside in. To get the most from this process, I recommend making wearable pieces one to two days ahead of the wear date, placing them in a suitably sized hydration chamber, and storing them in a cool, dark place. Ideally, this would be a professional floral cooler, kept between 34°F and 38°F [1°C and 3°C] with 80 to 95% relative humidity, but basements, root cellars, garages, and barns (within season) will do. Even a home refrigerator is suitable;

just take care to make sure your container is airtight (fruit and vegetables emit ethylene gas that can shorten the life of your flowers) and place the container in a zone that's been tested safe from freezing.

Floral installations are a bit more involved, but I enjoy comparing them to wearables. I see them as "corsages for a room," because they too are adornments that contribute a celebratory feeling to an event and are meant to be enjoyed only for the length of the party. Unlike centerpieces, after the celebration these big beauties typically go straight to the compost instead of home with guests. These artful requests are incredibly rewarding to create, but they require knowledge of the materials and engineering know-how—especially if you intend to design sustainably. I've learned over the years that when you use long-lasting, sturdy plant materials, you can create these fleeting designs with low or zero waste. Just as I

do with wearable work, I depend on sturdy, naturally dried or fresh reliables (see page 164) to execute these designs so they look great for the length of an event. With these hardworking materials as my primary elements, I can design largely water-free.

To create floral installations, I like to hang fresh materials from wire, twine, or fishing line, or tuck them directly into reusable chicken wire forms (I call them "burritos") without a water source. I view conventional hydration methods (floral foam, water tubes) as overkill, as these displays are typically asked to perform for just one night. The concept of designing water-free is viewed as blasphemy in some floral circles, but it is quickly gaining traction as the culture of floristry progresses and more and more designers are examining their choices and how they impact our health and the health of our environment. Dependence on single-use plastic hydration methods is on the way out, as more of us recognize that the end does not justify the means—art made from nature should not contribute to its demise. Single-use plastics not only rely on the fossil fuels that have led to climate change but also contribute to the waste stream.

Just like wearables, large floral pieces can be made in advance and treated with the hydration chamber method. I'll often design large installations in sections a day ahead, spray them with water, and cover them with a tarp or large garbage bags. The following day, they are hydrated and ready to go to their party.

In addition to reducing waste, water-free designing gives you a level of creative freedom you don't have with conventional design. These displays can hang, climb, or "grow," embellishing and beautifying any structure strong enough to support them. They ask both creator and viewers to pause and drink in their ephemeral beauty—to me, this pause is the very purpose of this art form.

DISPLAYING FLOWERS

VASES and VESSELS

In any arrangement, the flowers are certainly the star, but the success of a floral composition does depend on having a solid supporting foundation. As you begin your journey of floral discovery, you may be thinking of that collection of utilitarian vases gathering dust on a high shelf or cupboard. Maybe they were purchased over the years, or gifted to you, or arrived at your door as part of an arrangement from the local florist.

I will be bold enough to guess that most of them are not well loved or well used. I've always been a person who brings flowers as gifts when invited to dinner or a party, so over the years, I have seen many of these collections. The vases are usually made of thick, clear glass; they're typically cylindrical, with an awkward, in-between height. At 8 to 14 inches [20 to 35.5 cm], they are too short to support an effective statement piece and too tall for an appropriate centerpiece. Beyond the awkward height, these vases are often too narrow to allow the flowers to be displayed with any natural flair, instead scrunching the flower heads together.

These observations have prompted me to bring my floral gifts complete, vessel included. This makes for a much more meaningful gift and also doesn't require the recipient to pause the party and hastily rummage through their vessel stash.

So, what are the qualities of an appealing and useful vessel? For gifting and for my own use, I look to collect a variety of shapes and sizes that can serve three primary purposes: centerpiece design, statement piece design, and small space design.

CENTERPIECES

Centerpieces are meant to entice diners and welcome them to the table, to delight the senses and inspire rich conversation. In my mind, the flowers are as important as the food; however, they shouldn't distract from the experience of enjoying a meal. Florists generally categorize centerpieces in two ways: low and elevated. Low displays occupy the space below eye level (the industry standard is no higher than 14 inches [35.5 cm]), and elevated centerpieces occupy the space above eye level (typically above 30 inches [76 cm]). Remember the awkward vase height I mentioned earlier? When flowers are added to a vase that's more than 8 inches [20 cm] high, it's hard to avoid creating a composition that obstructs the diners' views across the table. It's likely we've all been at a dinner party where the centerpiece is finally removed from the table after people tire of craning their necks to see the people seated on the other side. To create welcoming centerpieces that will stay in place, reach for vases or vessels below 6 inches [15 cm] high. This gives you the vertical space you need to display your materials gracefully without compromising sight lines across the table. I much prefer the ease of designing low centerpieces, and for the home floral arranger, this is definitely the most approachable and appropriate design to explore first.

To begin building a vessel collection perfect for low centerpieces, you can certainly look for low vessels and vases meant for displaying flowers, but also consider soup and cereal bowls, footed compote bowls, and wide handleless cups, as they are often the perfect height and width. Consider building your design in a collection of bud vases like those shown in the Complementary Tablescape centerpiece on page 136, or

in a few matching fruit compotes like in the Garden Variety centerpiece on page 128. Also keep in mind that opaque vases made of materials such as pottery or metal are much more forgiving than clear glass, as they hide unruly or messy stems and design mechanics such as chicken wire or flower frogs. This especially helps new designers create a more polished composition. See the Resources section (page 169) for more details on some of my favorite vase sources.

STATEMENT PIECES

Statement pieces are dramatic, attention-grabbing displays typically arranged in a large vessel. They can be placed in any living space big enough to welcome them. In my home, I set these pieces on my entryway table, on a simple plinth in the living room, and sometimes, when I'm feeling fancy, in the bedroom. They can be very simple (a few branches in a tall vase always inspires) or more complex. For simple or spare arrangements,

rded Iris
germanica
Rimfire

Full Sun

45

SEDUM HYBRID
'Vera Jameson'

Donahue's
Clematis

'BUTTER AN
IRIS S

DURANDII
PERENNIAL
Bush type with rich, indigo-blue
flowers with white stamens.
Interesting cut flower.
HOW TO GROW:
Plant in sun or partial
shade. Grows 3-4 (1-1.2
m) vine. Shade roots to
keep soil cool and
moist. Pruning type 3

33

SUN TO PART SHADE
5-6 hours direct sun
Lady's Mantle
'Thriller'
PERENNIAL

SUMMER
BLOOM TIME

32

PERENNIAL

LADY'S MANTLE

Alchemilla mollis (vulgaris)

| SPRING | SUMMER | FALL |

*See back for more
information*

18

SNEEZEWEED
'Autumn Lollipop'

**Helenium
puberulum**
PERENNIAL
Unique lollipop-shaped
flowers are excellent for
late season color.
HOW TO GROW:
Plant in sun or part
shade 20-24" (51-61
cm) apart. Grows to
36" (91 cm) tall.

CRB0341

11

**Piccadilly™
Denim Blue**
DIASCIA
Spring is here! Accessorize your
containers and gardens.

**Partial Sun
Soleil Partiel**

6

**THEON
IA**
nodding
borne in
ender, very
ow

GROW:
sun or
inches
part.
12-16
30-41
tall.

Bearded Iris
Iris germanica
Siva Siva

Full Sun

**HIMALAYAN
CINQUEFOIL**
'Golden Starlit'

**Potentilla
atrosanguinea**
PERENNIAL
Bright flowers complement
silvery green foliage. Ideal
in rock gardens or
containers.
HOW TO GROW:
Plant in sun or part
shade 12" (30 cm)
apart. Grows to 12"
(30 cm) tall.

115209

VARIEGATED OREGANO

ORIGANUM VULGARE
'AUREUM VARIEGATA'

Height
6-8" (15-20cm)
Space
16" (40cm)

B
I

CARNATION
'Grenadin Yellow'

Dianthus

ANNUAL
'Chameleon'
Blueberry Scone

CRB0216

23

CALIBRACHOA

PERENNIAL

CENTAUREA MONTANA

tall slim vases will do. For displays that require more stems, look for vases that are 12 inches [30.5 cm] tall or more, and at least 6 inches [15 cm] wide. Two of my favorites for this type of arrangement appear in the following pages. Both of these beautiful handmade vessels stand about 13 inches [33 cm] tall and are about 9 inches [23 cm] wide at the middle. I reach for these two again and again because they have perfect round bellies and narrow necks. These qualities allow me to add a generous number of stems to the vessel at extreme angles. As I insert each stem into the vessel, the butt end of it finds a stopping point against the inner wall of the rotund middle. The insertion angle allows the stems above the rim to splay, giving me the freedom to create large displays with sweeping lines and a natural, airy form. For extra stem support and stability, you can fill these vessels with chicken wire, stones, or sand.

SMALL SPACES

I love to sprinkle small floral arrangements throughout the house, especially in the spring and summer when there are plenty of little treasures to bring in from the garden. I do this for my own pleasure and to add natural beauty, scent, and a sense of aliveness to the house for all to enjoy. I do this in the hope that my kids notice and find some delight in these little displays. It's especially fun to sprinkle these around when getting ready to welcome guests. I'll gather a collection of bud vases, tuck a few stems into each, and place them on the coffee table and side tables and next to the sink in the powder room. Sometimes, when I have a bit more time, I create little compositions arranged in petite bowls, sake cups, ramekins, walled dishes, or other small vessels. For these, I often reach for a small kenzan or pin frog to provide support for my materials.

SIMPLE DESIGN MECHANICS and TECHNIQUES

DESIGN MECHANICS

Over the years, humans have created a myriad of innovative ways to control the placement of flowers and foliage. Florists refer to these methods collectively as "mechanics." They are natural or human-made structures placed in or on vessels to hold materials just where the arranger wants them. The actual container for the arrangement can also serve as a mechanic as the internal structure allows the piece to be realized. Each arrangement will have its own set of needs, based on the characteristics of the natural materials you choose, the form and size of the composition, and its water needs. There is an appropriate mechanic for each unique composition. In my studio, I aim to use materials that are either durable and reusable or compostable, and this aim extends to the structures that support my stems. I'll share more on my favorite methods by grouping these useful frameworks into two categories: natural supports and human-made supports.

NATURAL SUPPORTS

I am not an expert on the matter, but I imagine that floral design supports made of natural materials found their way into the modern floral design lexicon after being popularized through the art of ikebana. In ikebana, innovative props called *hana kubari* are crafted out of branches, stems, leaves, roots, pods, vines, and any number of other strong, flexible, or supportive natural materials that suit themselves to manipulation. You may see a support made out of a collection of leathery leaves, a single branch, or a coil of vine like in the Reflecting Pool arrangement on page 57. These elements can be tucked snugly inside the walls of a container, slotted lengthwise and attached to the edge of a vase, coiled or lined up inside a shallow walled dish, or propped over a vessel. Flowers and foliage are then added to the composition, using these props as their anchor. When supportive frameworks created from natural elements are used outside of the ikebana school of design, they are often called "armatures." Both hana kubari and armatures can be purely functional or both functional and decorative. They can be purposely exposed and integral to the composition, like the Petite Armature design on page 60, or they can be tucked completely inside a vessel and used solely to provide structure for a design. Unlike hana kubari, armatures can also be human-made—which we'll discuss next.

HUMAN-MADE SUPPORTS

Successful floral compositions depend on a reliable supportive framework. The more complex or large the design becomes, the more its success depends on a solid starting point. Beyond supports crafted from natural materials, there are all kinds of human-made devices and media designed to stabilize flowers and make arranging them easier.

In this book, I'll outline the three methods I find the most approachable, sustainable, and applicable to current floral design: chicken wire forms, wire armatures, and kenzan or flower frogs. In my studio, these favorites add structure and stability to my arrangements and help me bring to life the designs in my head. All of these supportive frameworks are reusable and adaptable to many different design applications. However, each has qualities that lend them to specific design applications.

Chicken Wire Forms

If I had to choose one supportive framework to have in my studio, it would definitely be chicken wire. It's affordable, reusable, and infinitely useful in actualizing all manner of compositions—from simple centerpieces to large-scale floral installations. To use it as a support for a composition in a vessel, roll out an appropriate length—I typically measure twice the amount of the width of the vessel—and fold it in on itself to create a loose, multilayered orb, slightly larger than the volume of the vessel. The folds in the wire are important—as stems pass through, each layer provides a little more support to them, ultimately locking them securely in place. For deep vessels, simply tuck the orb inside, sink your hands into it, and pull it out toward the walls of the vessel to ensure it fills the space snugly. For shallow vessels, like the compote bowls in the Garden Variety arrangements on page 128, place a chicken wire orb in each vessel and secure with waterproof tape, floral bind wire, or twine. Add water and begin arranging your flowers. After the flowers have lived their life, shake them out of the orb and compost them. Wash your orbs with hot water and soap, then store them for future use.

Chicken wire is also used to take designs way beyond the vase— as in the Wall Flowers piece on page 152 or the sculptural Flower Tower piece on page 161. The basis for these larger installations is created with the chicken wire burritos described earlier—cylindrical wire tubes, in this case stuffed with sturdy dried materials. I make these by rolling out an appropriate length of wire, lining it with these materials, and rolling it up into a multilayered tube. I secure the tube with a twist of bind wire or a simple knot of twine every foot or so. These tubes become the design medium, providing a reliable structure into which stems can be easily and securely inserted. They offer structure and provide a basis for compositions, but they don't offer hydration, so you need to carefully select materials (see the Reliables list on page 164 for more) and make use of the hydration chamber method. See Caring for Your Cut Flowers (page 20) for more on material selection and water-free design.

Wire Armatures

Put simply, armatures are frameworks used to support the weight of materials in a composition. Armatures can be decorative—meant to be seen and contribute to the overall aesthetic of the design—or purely functional, meant to provide structure only, disappearing within the composition. In the floral design world, they are viewed as a somewhat advanced mechanic, not often taught to new students. However, they need not intimidate, as making these useful props can be simple and straightforward. I love the control that working with armatures gives me; I think they really are a wonderful method for new floral arrangers to experiment with.

There are many ways to create wire armatures. Many are made by meticulously crafting uniform webs or networks out of numerous interlocking wires; others are made simply, by manipulating a long length of wire into the form you desire. The latter appeals to me—these simple, uncontrived tangles of wire can be bent and shaped to create whatever you can dream up. They also appear more natural, mimicking the swirls and curves of vines and other plant material. To make an armature like this, simply use stem wrap tape to coat a length of malleable wire. I often use 18 gauge aluminum craft wire or spool wire from the hardware store. The length of the wire will depend on

how large and tightly coiled you want the resulting armature to be; I often use at least 10 feet [3 m] of wire to create mine. If stem wrap tape isn't available to you, consider painting the wire or wrapping it with yarn. See the Art Muse project on page 52 for an example of this type of armature.

The other way I like to create wire armatures is even simpler: cover a number of straight florist wires in stem wrap tape and secure them to the pins of a flower frog. Sink one end into the frog, get creative with the body of the wire, bending and guiding it into the position you desire, and sink the opposite end back into the pin frog. These wire loops supplement the frog, extending the support it offers to the materials within the composition. See the Petite Armature design on page 60 for more.

Flower Frogs and Kenzan

After much digging, I have come to the conclusion that all kenzan are flower frogs, but not all flower frogs are kenzan. Let's sort this out a bit, shall we? As with natural armatures, it's thought that the practice of ikebana is responsible for the invention of the first weighted, spiked flower supports. Kenzan *(sword mountain* or *needle mountain)* are sturdy, reusable disk-shaped props typically made with a heavy lead base and either steel or brass pins. These devices are secured to the bottom of vessels with floral putty, where their densely packed pins are used to hold natural materials in place. As I write this book, kenzan and flower frogs are experiencing quite a renaissance. As awareness of sustainable floral design practices increases, more and more people are turning away from the single-use design medium (flower foam) that took over the floral design landscape since its invention in the 1950s; now they are looking for reliable and reusable design mechanics. A minimal, spare design aesthetic is also gaining favor, and these time-honored props are the natural choice for such compositions. The origin of the term *flower frog* is a mystery, but it

seems to serve as an umbrella term for all manner of pottery, glass, and metal objects that are set in or fixed to the bottom of a vessel and serve to hold stems in place. It appears that the name *frog* gained popularity in the 1870s, when interest in Japanese design peaked in the West. Westerners were introduced to the ikebana style of design and began to playfully refer to the little metal creatures lurking under the water as "frogs."

The flower frog family is vast— there are metal pin frogs, wire hairpin frogs, glass disk frogs, metal cage frogs, and ceramic frogs. My favorite source for flower frogs and kenzan is the US company Floral Genius (retail sales are through Harmony Harvest Farm; see Resources, page 169). I reach for 3-inch [7.5 cm] metal pin holders and 3.5-inch [9 cm] hairpin holders for centerpiece work, and their 7/8-inch [about 2 cm] pin holder for petite satellite arrangements.

SETTING *the* SCENE

I imagine that most of my readers feel comfortable enough to tackle placing flowers in a vase, but I aim to offer ideas that will encourage you to try out larger and more complex floral displays.

Most of us don't have the sort of prop room that event florists have—full of decorative stands, stanchions, structures, arches, and all manner of foundational elements meant for showcasing floral compositions. Even so, we can still create impressive floral displays. I've purposely limited the props I used in this book, creating only with elements that I feel are available to most people.

To create a wall piece, consider starting with a natural vine armature like the one in the Studio Scene piece on page 73, or a chicken wire form like the Wall Flowers piece on page 152. A few discreetly placed nails are all you need to secure these wall art compositions in place. To create a hanging display, consider making a base structure by tying branches together as in the floating Flower Shower arch on page 149. The branch "skeleton" for this design is hung from a strong overhead support beam with heavy gauge fishing line. Another reliable way to create a hanging display is to attach natural materials to a weight-bearing fixture, as in the Aerial Amaryllis design on page 157. Building from an existing structural or architectural element in a space makes the construction process easier and adds focus to the design.

To create freestanding or climbing floral installations, always start with a solid inner structure. I like to create the basis for sculptural standing pieces like the Flower Tower on page 161 by securing an inexpensive steel grounding rod (purchased at the hardware store) into a sturdy base such as a patio umbrella or Christmas tree stand. Chicken wire is added to the rod to provide a place to add stems. As with any creative endeavor, experimentation and practice will lead to confidence. Let the ideas in this book inspire you to use what you have around you to create your own unique compositions.

WIRING

I've purposely kept the techniques in this book simple, low fuss, and approachable, but I couldn't resist including a few slightly more advanced wire work projects. Straight floral wire is a staple in my studio; this mechanism allows the designer to support delicate stems, manipulate materials, maximize ingredients, and create little works of wearable floral art. You may not yet be familiar with it, but I promise it is easy to work with. To create the projects in this book, you need only a pair of needle-nose pliers from the hardware store, florist stem wrap tape, and two types of wire, available at most craft stores. To create the floral earrings on page 91, I used gold-filled 20 gauge jewelry spool wire, and for the crown on page 92 and the Simply Strung projects on pages 86 and 88, I used 20 gauge straight floral wire. I decided to focus on projects that employ a simple threading method to keep them approachable to most. If you can string beads, you can thread flowers! See the following section for more on how to work with wire to create the projects in this book.

HOOK METHOD WIRING

1. Prepare the florets you plan to work with a day in advance by cutting them from their stems and treating them in the hydration chamber.
2. Prepare your wires by bending one end of each into a little narrow hook using needle-nose pliers.
3. Thread the first bloom onto the wire, petal end first, taking care to guide the wire through the body of the bloom so it pierces the very center.
4. Pull the bloom down gently until it makes contact with the hook and rests securely on it. Ensure that this first

bloom is locked in place before continuing.

5. Continue to carefully thread florets onto the wire, nestling each tubular end snugly into the bloom end of the previous one. Stop when the wire is mostly full; leave a little empty handling space to attach or secure each wire into place within the design

6. Follow photos below for guidance on wiring, proceding clockwise from top left.

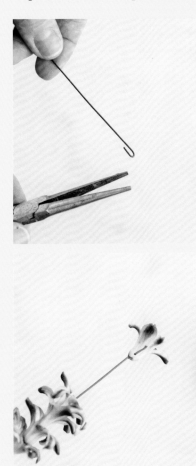

FLOWERS FOR ME

SIMPLE PROJECTS TO
BRING JOY, MINDFULNESS,
AND BEAUTY TO YOUR DAYS

FLOWER YOURSELF

I've mentioned that I buy flowers for myself regularly. I buy them not only because they add life and inspiration to my living space, but also because I feel compelled to regularly demonstrate my support of flower growers (especially local growers) in a tangible way. I'm especially charmed by unusual flowers or less common varieties, like these incredible 'Black Hero' tulips grown by Luella Acres (see Resources, page 169). When I see flowers like this—flowers that are almost a bit challenging to the general public—I snatch them up greedily and take them home. I feel drawn to the odd, unfamiliar, and unconventional, and I'm passionate about championing them. They demand our attention and ask us to pause our busyness and take note of their striking beauty. Pink, red, or yellow tulips are wonderful, but they're almost mundane and easy to overlook. These otherworldly obsidian beauties, on the other hand, really captivate.

TIPS:

- To ensure long-lasting and tidy tulip arrangements, remove extraneous leaves when preparing your blooms. I typically remove all leaves that are too large to remain upright in the arrangement. Pull each leaf down until the connection point to the stem becomes visible, and carefully tear it horizontally until you free it from the stem. Use a sharp florist (or paring) knife to gently shave any remaining leaf fragments from the stem.

- I've created a little floral environment for myself with these tulips by pressing them into a collection of metal pin frogs. For a longer-lasting display, simply pop each frog into a reservoir of water. Little dishes, trays, or bowls make the perfect receptacles for these uncomplicated compositions.

- I am lucky to live in a place with a robust community of local growers and many outlets for procuring their flowers. This is especially precious in the early spring, when greenhouse-grown beauties like these tulips become available before my garden flowers arrive to banish the winter doldrums. Consider joining a floral CSA or subscription to support your local growers and guarantee an early spring mood boost each year.

FLORAL SUPPORT

Hyacinths are one of my very favorite early spring flowers. As
soon as they are available, I bring them indoors to cheer me up
and reassure me that warm days are near. I love to display them,
but their weak, fleshy stems present a bit of a design challenge.
I like to create floral supports for flowers like these out of sturdy
materials like these tallow berry branches. Just a few slim but
strong branches provide structure to nodding stems and keep
them in their intended position. I purposely keep these arrangements simple so I can create enough with one bunch to scatter
arrangements throughout the house, spreading the heady scent of
spring through every room. Create a slim vertical arrangement like
this one, designed in my favorite footed Noe Kuremoto vase (see
Resources, page 171), or a wider composition like the one shown in
a suiban-style shallow dish on page 85.

TIPS:

- Start with a clean, dry kenzan or frog and a low, wide vessel (I like to use walled dishes or bowls). Measure out a ribbon of floral putty from the roll, equivalent to your frog's circumference. Press it to the underside of your frog, completely tracing the perimeter of the base. Put the frog into the vessel and press down, twisting to secure the frog in place.

- Stagger two or three frogs in the vessel so each bloom has a chance to shine. Choose airy supportive materials that complement the focal flowers instead of competing for attention.

- When using shallow vessels, be sure to regularly check the water level of the arrangement. I like to bring these guys to the kitchen sink and flush out the old water as I replace it with fresh. This keeps the vessel free of bacterial buildup, allowing me to enjoy the flowers for as long as possible.

FLORAL MEDITATION

Collecting ingredients for this simple and satisfying presentation includes a walking meditation. Select a low tray or vessel, head outdoors, and walk slowly through your yard, garden, or any available green space, snipping attractive bits of foliage, florets, or blooms that you find. If you don't have access to a green space, purchase herbs, plants, and flowers at a local garden center or farmers' market. Allow the process of selecting materials to bring your thoughts to the present moment. This feels so luxurious to me: slowing down enough to snip materials thoughtfully, appreciating the colors, textures, and details in every ingredient. Once your materials are ready, add water to your vessel, and set them afloat in the dish. Set the dish in a place in your home where you'll see it regularly—a bathroom or kitchen counter—and allow it to provide brief moments of beauty and calm throughout your days.

TIPS:

- An idea this simple hardly requires instruction. This is exactly why it is so lovely: it's available to everyone, from small children to accomplished gardeners or seasoned florists. It's also a great way to do more with less—to enjoy flowers in your home without cutting too much from any one plant.

- As you enjoy your display, take care to change the water regularly, and remove any blooms that are past their prime. Interestingly, some materials last a long time displayed this way, while others break down quickly due to the constant contact with water. A few flowers that have worked well for me include clematis, pansies, hellebore, allium, tulip, ranunculus, bougainvillea, nigella, scabiosa, and chrysanthemum.

ART MUSE

I love taking inspiration from art objects, like this fantastical stack of painted Avery Williamson cubes (see Resources, page 170). I take cues from the energetic lines, patterns, and collection of colors in her art and allow them to influence my home decor and color choices; they also inspire my floral displays. Clean, simple arrangements become elevated when they interact thoughtfully with the art. In these pages, enjoy a few simple examples of how art and flowers can play together. First, a few stems of deeply veined brunnera foliage and freckled 'Roselily Sita' Oriental lilies from the garden vibe well with their cube partner. Repetition in color, pattern, and form make the complete collection more interesting than its parts. Second, an airy white wire armature repeats the dynamic white lines in the artwork, and the delicate young hops vine and white gaura blooms speak to the playful swirls and patterns in the cube. Place arrangements like this someplace where you spend time working or thinking—like a home office—to help inspire creativity.

TIPS:

- Both of these arrangements benefit from the inclusion of artful vessels. The form and pattern of these Noe Kuremoto vessels harmonize with the other design elements, elevating the composition and contributing to its overall success.

- In the first composition, I wanted to draw attention to the burgundy freckling and amber markings on the rose lilies, so I removed all of the distracting lily foliage, gathered my stems together in a little bundle—placing the lilies above the brunnera leaf—and secured them with twine, then tucked them into the vase. The petite partner arrangement is simply a few stems set into a pin frog.

• To make the airy armature that supports the second composition, I simply used stem wrap tape to coat a length of malleable wire. I used 18 gauge aluminum craft wire and white stem wrap tape, but you could also experiment with painting the wire or coating it in decorative washi tape. The wire length will depend on how large and tightly coiled you want the resulting armature to be—mine required 12 feet [3.6 m] of wire to create.

REFLECTING POOL

Three petite, innocent-looking luffa gourd plants that I bought at
the farmers' market this spring exploded into a wonderful chaotic
mass of vines and fruit that completely overwhelmed my vegetable
garden by summer. I planted the luffas so I could harvest the fruit,
but I also found so much enjoyment in designing with the plentiful
sturdy vines. The vines scamper up anything strong enough to
support them by sending out swirling, spring-like tendrils that
anchor the vine as it climbs. They almost seem sentient—reaching,
searching, and creating a path to the sunlight they need. The tendril-
filled vines make wonderful natural armatures, as beautiful as
they are functional. Here and in the following pages, spectacular
passionflower blooms from Graye's Greenhouse (see Resources,
page 169) shine as the focus of a simple composition supported by
these charming vines. On the next page, a swirl of luffa vine is set
into a deep bowl-shaped metal vase. Late summer cobaea vine and
penstemon flowers are arranged within its swirls.

TIPS:

- To make a natural vine armature, clip a long length of vine from the plant, taking care to preserve as much of the delightful tendril material as possible. Remove the foliage, and curl the vine over itself until you form a loosely layered coil. Tuck it into a straight-sided vessel and adjust the armature so its coils are taut against the walls of the vessel. Use the armature as a support for delicate foliage, vines, and blooms.

- If luffa plants are not in your garden plans (though they really should be), consider creating natural coiled armatures out of other vines such as wild grape, ivy, or hops, or out of flexible branches such as curly willow, contorted filbert, or weeping birch.

PETITE ARMATURE

I love creating airy, monobotanical displays (that is, featuring a single species or variety) with delicate flowers such as these beautiful blue Chinese forget-me-nots from Marilla Field & Flora (see Resources, page 169). I was lucky to find these flowers on the farm during a late-season visit. An unusually warm October allowed me to catch them in an interesting transitional phase between flower and seed. I arranged these wispy stems in a Holly Chapple compote fitted with a metal pin frog supplemented with an armature of tape-covered florist wires. As I added each tender stem to the arrangement, I propped and supported them with the armature loops, securing each in perfect position within the composition.

TIPS:

- To make the wire loops that create this armature, first use stem wrap tape to cover straight florist wires. This allows you to choose the armature color and also prevents the wires from rusting under the waterline. After preparing the wires, secure one end of each into the frog spikes, make loose loops with its length, and secure the other end into the frog.

- If you are still gaining confidence in your floral arranging skills, consider using simple armatures like this to achieve the overall form you intend to create. Wire is much more forgiving than floral material—you can bend and shape it into whatever form you desire. Once the wire skeleton of your form is set, follow that shape as you add your floral material. Having an inner structure as a guide will ease your effort.

AROMATHERAPY

The modest herb garden outside my kitchen door provides me with all sorts of perfumed treasures, including mint, lavender, artemisia, sage, thyme, lemon verbena, and rosemary. I love to snip bits of this or that to make tea or use in cooking, always pausing to stroke the leaves of each plant to set their scent free. I also love to arrange with herbs, setting the arrangements in the restful spaces in my home. Here, a collection of garden herbs mingles with love-in-a-puff vine, hosta flowers, and blooming autumn clematis to make a long-lasting display full of delicious scents.

TIPS:

- If you don't have space for an herb garden, consider starting a small container garden on your patio or in a well-lit space in your home. Inexpensive herb bundles can also often be found at farmers' markets.

- To get more aesthetic enjoyment from the herbs you use for cooking, consider lining your kitchen countertop with a number of petite vases. Display the herbs that you buy at the market or snip from the garden in these, like little bouquets. This allows you to enjoy a view of your harvest, rather than just chucking them into the refrigerator. Also, tender herbs such as basil, dill, and cilantro much prefer room temperature to the chill of a home fridge.

COLOR STUDY

An easy way to create a cohesive little collection of elements is to focus on color. As you build a vase collection, for instance, look for vases that will play well together. Currently, I look for white vases and vases in shades of pale greenish blue. It gives focus to the hunt and creates an assemblage of components that work well together. Here, a selection of my blue vases holds a mostly monochromatic gathering of flowers, foliage, and berries collected from my yard, neighborhood, and a local floral shop. My practice of paying close attention to how colors play together always sparks ideas.

TIPS:

- To quickly amass a cohesive vessel collection, consider applying the same color paint to inexpensive vases you find at flea markets, secondhand stores, or garage sales. An eclectic mix of sizes and shapes becomes instantly harmonious, united by color.

- Consider creating a color study flat lay (a photograph or painting of assorted objects arranged on a flat surface) of your own by collecting interesting materials from your environment and arranging them on a display board. I love to document little treasure collections this way, whether to keep the photos or share them online. Flowers are fleeting—this is a way to enjoy them long after they've passed.

STUDIO SCENE

A tangle of dried smilax vine (*Smilax rotundifolia*) becomes a sprawling wall armature perfect for drying a haul of ash seed clusters. I love to dry seedpods, foliage, grasses, and flowers for later use, but I struggle to find space for them in my home studio. It was quite satisfying to create a hanging display as beautiful as it is functional. Smilax vine is perfect for this use—it's strong and flexible, with tons of grabby, wispy lateral branches that act as hooks for hanging materials easily. If smilax isn't available to you, consider using grapevine, elaeagnus vine (*Elaeagnus pungens*), young bittersweet, Virginia creeper, or spent sweet autumn clematis.

TIPS:

- To make the most of my small space and create an interesting display, I decided to attach the vine to the wall and guide it up overhead. I placed one cup hook in the ceiling and two discreet nails in the wall. I used paper-covered bind wire to secure the vine to the hook and nails.

- Smilax is incredibly moldable, thanks to the plethora of miniature lateral branches on each main stem. I tucked and twisted the vine and shaped it into the form I wanted, using these laterals to achieve my desired shape. Use twine or bind wire to help create your desired form, especially if you're using a vine without such plentiful lateral branching.

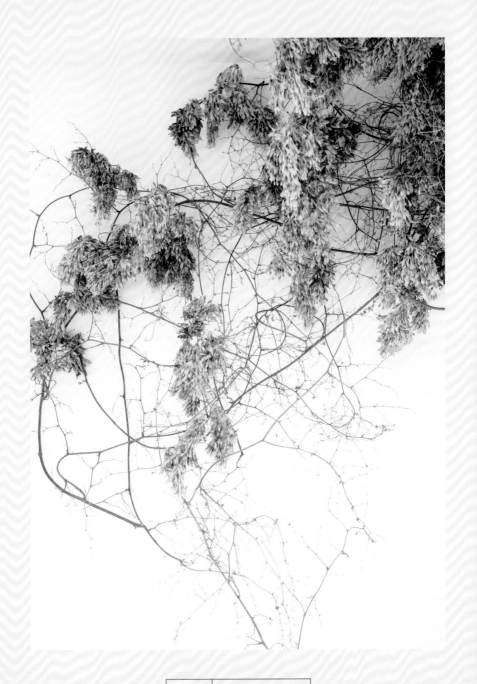

FLORAL GALLERY

My love for flowers is such that I document nearly every flower
that enters the studio. I've done this ever since I've had a decent
phone camera, about seven or eight years. For a flower aficionado
like me, the simple act of capturing their images brings joy, but
there is another reason I maintain this practice. I gather these
images to keep me inspired, share proof of the incredible flowers
I work with every day, and most important, record seasonal
findings. It's helpful to have a record of what blooms when,
especially when you live in a place with a short growing season
like I do. I've grown to love these simple iPhone snaps—so much
so that I decided to have my favorites printed so I could display
them on my studio wall. I love that this inexpensive idea can turn
single blooms and humble phone pics into art.

TIPS:

- A good source of natural light is key to taking quality phone photos. I shoot my flowers against a white wall adjacent to a west-facing window. On sunny days the light is perfect in the early morning and late afternoon. I stand a few feet away from the wall, hold my subject in my nondominant hand, and pivot toward the window until the flower is bathed in natural light. I hold my phone in my other hand, with the camera flipped toward me so I can see what the camera sees before I take a snap. The pivoting and previewing make fast work of documenting each flower—especially helpful when I bring in a large haul.

- Consider creating collections based on color, like my golden-hued gallery, or based on season. Display them simply so you can swap collections out easily as the seasons (or your moods) change throughout the year.

FLOWERS FOR FRIENDS

ARRANGEMENTS TO
SPREAD JOY AND CULTIVATE
CONNECTION WITH LOVED ONES

PERENNIAL PRESENT

The best gift a flower lover can receive is a blooming plant that returns year after year. Early spring perennials like these icy blue muscari (grape hyacinth) are among the first flowers to appear each year, making them that much more precious. A vase of flowers is a lovely gift, of course, but consider what a gift of bulbs could offer. Each year when spring returns, your gifts will emerge and bloom, reminding your friend of your thoughtfulness.

TIPS:

- For a really generous gift, tuck a selection of bulbs and a pin frog into a handmade vessel, like an earthy, textural Noe Kuremoto suiban. With this complete package, the lucky recipient will have everything they need to enjoy the flowers you gifted them when they emerge in the spring.

- An assortment of bulbs like the collection of scilla, muscari, narcissus, hyacinth, and fritillaria (opposite) makes an especially thoughtful gift because they don't all bloom at once, thus increasing the enjoyment window.

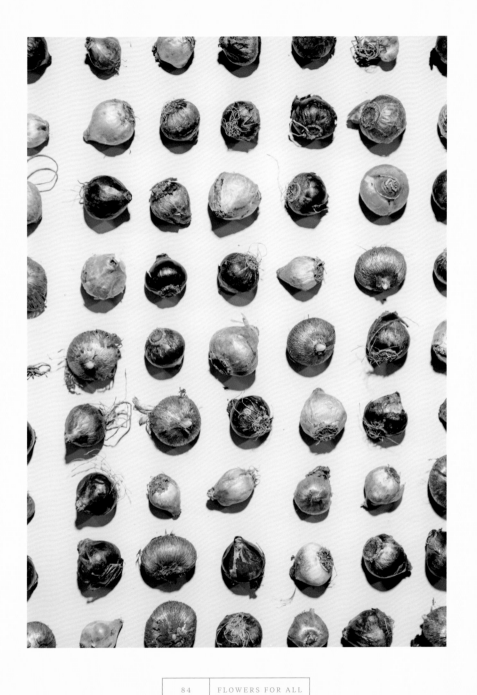

SIMPLY STRUNG

My career as a florist began when a friend asked me to arrange the flowers for her wedding. That innocent request sparked an insatiable passion. I know I am not the only flower-loving, vaguely artistic person who's been asked to do this, so here I offer a simple method for creating a bridal bouquet with impressive results. If you've ever threaded beads on string, you can create this shower bouquet. Best part is, it doubles as an over-the-top floral headpiece—what fashionista wouldn't want to wear their bouquet to their reception? All that's needed to create this artful cascade are a handful of 20 gauge straight floral wires, stem wrap tape, and a generous amount of sturdy bead-like florets. I used vibrant blue hyacinth—one stem's worth of florets created one strung strand.

TIPS:

- To make a bouquet of this size, you will need approximately 30 stems of tubular, bell, or cup-shaped flowers. Other flowers that work well include agapanthus, tuberose, gladiola, daffodil, fritillaria, and double tulips.

- When creating your wire strands, stack blooms on the wire, leaving 4 inches [10 cm] of empty space at the end. Gather the empty wire ends in your hand and bundle them with stem wrap tape. Bend the bundle to create a gentle arc-shaped handle. Working with the bloom strands, bend and coax them into an overall rounded shape, creating dynamic lines and a pleasing composition.

TRUMPET BEADS

Everyday daffodils become golden trumpet beads with their outer petals removed. The flowers' inner trumpets are actually very sturdy and long-lasting, perfect for creating expressive, wired wearables. The same simple threading technique was used to create these delightful spring earrings as well as the fantastical headpiece on page 92. The frilly earrings make a lovely gift for any flower lover, and the headpiece will be the talk of any spring festivity.

TIPS:

- See the wiring instructions on page 36 for more on how to create these playful earrings. Stack as many trumpets as you like, but be sure to leave a bit of empty wire on the end to attach to an ear wire.

- All that's needed to make the golden headpiece on page 92 is a handful of 20 gauge straight floral wires, stem wrap tape, a simple metal headband, and fifty to sixty stems of daffodils. The same technique is used as the earrings— just repeated with longer wires. After the wires are stacked with blooms, use stem wrap tape to attach them, one by one, to the metal headband.

ARTFUL OFFERING

The best of the early spring flower market mingles together in this punchy arrangement for a friend. I look forward to the narcissus crop each year and love them all—the petite multiheaded jonquils, the ruffled doubles, and even the commonplace yellows—they are full of personality and good cheer. A few stems of cupped ranunculus add interest to the composition and play nicely with the form of the raawii compote vase (see Resources, page 171) from the Museum of Modern Art. This generous offering includes the delightful vessel; the flowers within are secured in a metal pin frog. My hope is that this encourages the recipient to create floral art in this vessel again and again.

TIPS:

- If you are still gaining comfort with floral arranging, consider focusing on monochromatic compositions. Color is the most powerful element of design—working within a tight palette will help you create a cohesive, pleasing design.

- I love to gift flowers as a package, complete with a beautiful vessel and useful design mechanic. This thoughtful presentation allows the recipient to enjoy the flowers right away without having to hunt for a vase or fuss with on-the-spot arranging.

AVOCADO INSPIRATION

I love finding muses in everyday objects. When you begin opening your mind to creative inspiration, you will notice beauty everywhere. Large arrangements make an artful and thoughtful gift for a housewarming or when celebrating the opening of a friend's new business. This arrangement was inspired by an avocado. Matte black and textured on the outside, creamy and pale green within— they are beautiful little objets d'art. They inspired me to fill my treasured black clay Noe Kuremoto "Tsubo" vessel with a collection of expressive avocado-green *Fritillaria persica* from Grateful Gardeners (see Resources, page 169), fluffy cherry branches from the yard, and a cluster of grapes purchased at the grocery store. This display makes a wonderful entryway piece that welcomes guests in and just asks to be touched—or plucked.

TIPS:

- One key to creating a stunning statement piece is finding a suitable vessel. Look for a tall, heavy vase with a narrow neck and full belly. This shape lends itself well to a naturally sprawling composition. Create year-round with a selection of blooming branches, raspberry vines, rose hips, or even dried ornamental grasses or wildflowers.

- To transport a big baby like this, place the completed arrangement in a low box and tuck it in snugly with newspaper. Place it on your car seat and belt it in, positioning the lap belt to secure the box and placing the shoulder strap around the back of the car seat to ensure it doesn't crush the flowers.

SUMMER STILL LIFE

I am a florist, but I consider members of the entire plant kingdom—and the kingdom of fungi—to be fair game. Fruits and vegetables are as inspiring and beautiful as flowers, and they too deserve a place in the vase. Every trip to the farmers' market or grocery store, every walk around the veggie garden is an opportunity for inspiration. Here, a collection of Japanese eggplant that I found too beautiful to just eat are arranged with unripe cherry tomatoes from the garden, sweet potato vine, elderflower bracts, and nicotiana blooms. I chose the materials for their form and color, but later paused and realized with satisfaction that the veggies (the nicotiana is too) are all members of the nightshade family. Maybe that's why they play together so well? Create a still life like this to delight dinner party guests or as an artful offering to a fellow gardenista.

TIPS:

- To create this piece, I began with a metal art display stand with a slim upright rod and 4-inch [10 cm] diameter base. I placed metal pin frogs on the base and set it into my Black Wing Clay compote vase (see Resources, page 171). The eggplant were simply threaded onto the rod, and the other materials secured into the frogs. The rod lent support to the tangle of tomatoes in the focal area of the composition.

- Edible materials are more fleeting than cut flowers, so take care to treat your fruit, vegetable, and fungi materials gently so you can make proper use of them after they serve as a display. I typically use edibles in still-life pieces for short-term party purposes.

DAHLIA DRAMA

This striking composition was made days before the first frost of the season. A foggy morning walk through Marilla Field & Flora's field inspired me to celebrate the last of the season's dahlias simply, by pairing them with soaring stems of overgrown 'Green Mist' ammi (*Ammi majus*, also called "bishop's lace" or "false Queen Anne's lace"). It was interesting to learn that as the days shorten, the ball dahlias become more and more eager for pollination, opening up faster to reveal their golden pollen-rich centers. Flower farmer friends consider these "blown" dahlia blossoms flawed and too open to sell, but I find them even more enthralling. When paired with nearly spent ammi from the field, the composition evokes the drama of fall.

TIPS:

- I fitted this incredible "elliptical trophy cup" vase from floral designer Tara Douglass (see Resources, page 171) with a large, loosely layered orb of chicken wire. The deep vase anchored the wire well, allowing me to easily place the tall, reaching ammi and the top-heavy nodding dahlia stems.

- This composition is simple and the ingredient list short—the drama here is created by the use of negative space. When working on any arrangement, be conservative as you cut stems, always trying out the full length of an ingredient before trimming it further.

WREATH PARTY

The decorations for a Friendsgiving gathering become parting gifts as the guests leave for the evening. These simple monobotanical wreaths were made a few days before the party and hung on the wall as a charming backdrop. The ash seed clusters, hydrangea, kangaroo paw, and yarrow were harvested and dried throughout the summer, and the heuchera foliage and blackberry lily pods were gathered from the garden. The privet, beautyberry, and blackberry lily wreaths are the perfect gifts for plant lovers, as the berries contain seeds that can be germinated. I love the idea of offering a gift that can live on in a friend's garden.

TIPS:

- For the wreath, begin with a reliable form. I used a collection of metal floral hoops from a craft store and made a few of my own with wire from the hardware store. If making your own, choose a gauge that is malleable enough to form by hand, but sturdy enough to maintain its shape under the weight of the plant material.

- To attach sturdy materials such as berry branches and yarrow, reach for 22-gauge spool wire. For tender-stemmed ingredients, like the heuchera foliage and hydrangea, secure with stem wrap tape. For speed, portion your plant material into easy-to-grab, evenly sized "bouquets." Place one bouquet on the wreath form and secure the stem ends to the form with three passes of wire or tape. Place the next bouquet over the stem ends of the last and secure. Repeat until the wreath is complete. Attach a discreet wire loop to the back of the wreath form for hanging.

CELEBRATORY SPIRAL

One of the most valuable floral design skills is the spiral bouquet method. Also called the hand-tied or Dutch bouquet, the technique is simple, but it does require a bit of patience and practice. Once you've mastered it, you can deftly unify loose stems, quickly creating lush, shapely, celebratory bouquets with slim waists and elegantly swirled stems. These bouquets are ideal for gifting, as they are perfectly prepped to pop into a vase. They also make lovely wedding bouquets and tidy farmers' market bunches. Here, a selection of citrus-hued heirloom mums from Harmony Harvest Farm combines to make a charismatic bouquet ready to be welcomed with open arms.

TIPS:

- To make a spiral bouquet, prepare your materials by removing any obtrusive foliage and laying them out on your workspace. Add a few stems to your dominant hand, stem ends facing your body. Add a few more stems to your hand, then give the bunch a quarter turn. Continue to add stems to your hand, laying them over the last few at the same angle, giving a quarter turn with every few additions. Hold onto the stems loosely, using mainly your thumb and middle finger. As you work, the bouquet will start to take shape; the binding point beneath your fingers will be slim and organized, and the flower heads above will fan out to create an abundant dome.

- After your bouquet is complete, secure the binding point with a slim belt of twine or bind wire. Trim the stems evenly—a well-balanced spiral bouquet should be able to stand on its own!

FALL FRUITS

This festive, fruit-filled tablescape makes a warm, welcoming centerpiece for a special harvest season family dinner. I love the repetition in round forms—late season apples from our tree play well with cheery clusters of crabapple and the berries on the swirly bittersweet vine from the farmers' market. The design may look intricate, but it is easily crafted thanks to the tubular branch-stuffed chicken wire garland foundation within. I began by tucking dried ash seed clusters into the sturdy garland base until the wire was roughly covered. Next I placed groupings of crabapple branch, cutting each stem short to allow the fruit to spill forward like tassels. Lacy dill blooms and bittersweet vine add an ethereal, airy finishing layer to this collection of seasonal elements.

TIPS:

- Chicken wire, twine, and a collection of sturdy branch material are all you need to create your own garland base. (See the Chicken Wire Forms section on page 30 for more.)

- The best thing about this design is its adaptability. You can use this same method to create spectacular mantel pieces, swags, front porch garlands, or artful wall pieces. Consider moving this fall dinner centerpiece to the mantel and enjoying it throughout the winter.

- By selecting long-lasting ingredients, this garland required no maintenance and looked perfectly fresh for over twelve days. Lean on materials with lasting power to create compositions that can be part of more than one seasonal celebration.

FLOWERS FOR ALL

GORGEOUS
PRESENTATIONS TO ENHANCE
ANY GATHERING

BLOOM ROOM

This impressive yet uncomplicated installation of electric yellow forsythia transformed the wall in my humble dining room into an engaging floral artwork—almost like living wallpaper. The branches were gathered from my backyard and from the neighbor (with permission). I added a water tube to each and hung them on the wall using a bit of wire and adhesive hooks. This simple approach resulted in a captivating, lively display for a special early spring dinner. Any slender branch with attractive blooms, berries, or foliage in quantity will work. Other materials that lend themselves well to this design include blooming branches such as cherry, apple, or pear; fruited branches and vines such as crabapple, rose hips, or holly; and delicate foliage such as willow, bamboo, or birch.

TIPS:

- This composition is best made on the day of the party. Water tubes don't hold that much water, so after installation, be sure to check water levels at least once a day. To create a seemingly effortless composition, look for clear water tubes that disappear within the design. I used 4-inch [10 cm] Aquatubes from Syndicate Sales (see Resources, page 171).

- For a permanent installation, consider designing with interesting bare branches such as contorted filbert, or tall dried ornamental grasses harvested from the garden in autumn.

GARDEN VARIETY

"Uncool" garden center flowers in punchy colors get the attention they deserve in this early summer runner centerpiece. Here, geranium, marigold, nasturtium, and lady's mantle from my garden and yarrow and ranunculus from local farms express themselves in airy arrangements held in yellow raawii Strøm bowl vases. Heirloom tomatoes from the farmers' market provide another serving of red and add zest to this seasonal display. The bright pops of color bring instant cheer to the tablescape, encouraging a sense of joy and playfulness. This presentation is perfect for a special summer dinner party with fellow garden lovers and foodies.

TIPS:

- I love designing with "ordinary" garden center plants. Geraniums are a favorite, as they are so prolific, blooming from last frost to first. Consider keeping several of these hardworking plants on your patio to snip from all summer long.

- Inexpensive elements such as these yellow melamine plates and stemmed coupe glasses get a boost when paired with my treasured Strøm vases. Gather elements based on color to create a cohesive tablescape out of unlikely companions.

SPRING SCENE

Unlike home gardeners, many flower growers pull their tulip bulbs out of the ground each season after they bloom. New bulbs are planted each year to guarantee strong, showy cut flowers. When I'm lucky enough to get bulb-on flowers, I love to display them in unexpected ways. Here, I created a simple wall gallery with a selection of ruffled 'Verona' double tulips from Marilla Field & Flora. A few varieties of narcissus from my garden filled out the display. This wall art piece made a charming focal point for a spring cocktail party, and because I'm not growing tulips to sell, I popped these babies into my garden after the celebration. I'll have to wait until next spring to see what they have to offer.

TIPS:

- I used paper clips and petite adhesive hooks to create this wall display. Attach the hooks to the wall, placing them thoughtfully to create a pleasing overall design. Open up a paper clip, forming an S shape. Use the bottom half of the S to hook into the bulb and use the top half to hang the bulb onto its anchor point.

- Another favorite way to display bulb-on tulips is to secure them directly into metal open frogs, roots and all, then set them in shallow dishes of water. I love adding these earthy elements to spring centerpieces.

COMPLEMENTARY TABLESCAPE

This spare collection of purply elements came alive when I moved it from my white dining room to this spot in front of my punchy amber wall. When we think of elements in our environment as part of a composition, we can transform relatively simple or calm displays into energetic interplays of color. I gathered the ingredients for this modern centerpiece from a favorite local farm stand, the flower growers' market, and my own garden. I chose a narrow palette— nearly all purple/black save for the soft bluish-lavender tweedia (a South American milkweed). I kept the vases soft so they'd blend into the white tabletop. There is nothing complicated here—simply the magnetism that colors across the color wheel have for each other.

TIPS:

- All visual artists benefit from a working knowledge of color theory. I keep a color wheel in my studio to inspire ideas, and I look to books like Josef Albers's *Interaction of Color* to stretch my imagination.

- When playing with a complementary color scheme, look for elements with both colors, like these delightful heirloom tomatillos from Slow Farm (see Resources, page 170).

PETAL PLAY

This lighthearted, exuberant display may not technically qualify as a floral design, but it is my favorite design of late. The process of removing the petals from the flower heads and sprinkling them onto the tabletop in layers was extremely meditative and satisfying. With each layer, new patterns and color interactions emerged— similar to the experience of layering paint onto a canvas. Create a petal-covered table to display desserts or place cards at an event, draw attention to a focal arrangement, or as an extravagant living tablecloth for a playful dinner party.

TIPS:

- My excitement prompted me to completely cover the table here, but my mom tells me this is not an appropriate scenario for dining. Consider sprinkling the petals down the center of a long dining table, creating a dense ribbon of color more suitable for "proper" place settings.

- Boost the longevity of flower petals by treating them in the hydration chamber. I freed these flowers from their stems three days in advance, popped them into sealable plastic bags, sprayed them with water, and stored them in a safe nook in my home refrigerator. In my testing, marigold petals stored this way beautifully for two weeks. For more on the hydration chamber method, see page 22.

- Flower petals, particularly sturdy and forgiving marigold petals, are a natural choice for confetti.

GARDEN GATHERING

A scattering of petite white vessels holding garden elements in shades of green creates a cohesive runner centerpiece for a late summer brunch. This may be my favorite way to compose: stepping out my back door into the garden to hunt for interesting bits that might play well together. Here, brunnera, hosta, nasturtium, lungwort, Japanese forest grass, artemisia, luffa gourd tendrils, and lupine are presented unpretentiously alongside clusters of immature currant tomatoes and stark white mushrooms from a local grocer. The calm palette welcomes guests in and makes them feel comfortable; the inclusion of unusual elements keeps them engaged.

TIPS:

- I am lucky enough to have many independent grocers in my area. All carry interesting, unusual produce. I love to incorporate these elements into my work—and the best part is, I can cook them for dinner later.

- These mushrooms stood up on their own, making them a wonderful, effortless design element. For mushrooms that need support, consider using hairpin flower frogs or small bowls to display them.

FLOWER SHOWER

Three dynamic ingredients make up this artful floating arch installation: bittersweet branches, cool blue porcelain berries, and lavender lisianthus. I began by crafting a supportive canopy out of the bittersweet branches. I wired them together, crossing them and attaching them with bind wire to form a wide, sturdy C-shaped structure. I hung the canopy from two supportive points on the ceiling with a strong invisible hanging wire. I attached (and sometimes simply hung) the rest of the bittersweet vine from the canopy to achieve an attractive arch shape. From there, I moved on to the porcelain vine, layering it into the bittersweet structure. I used small twists of wire here and there to secure the vine in place. Last, I added the lisianthus flowers by simply hanging them from the bittersweet branches. A single lisianthus has a branching configuration, typically consisting of two or three blooming heads and several lateral stems with immature blooms. I trimmed off the laterals, retaining just 1 inch [2.5 cm] or so of length to create natural V-shaped hooks for the flowers. These little hooks made fast work of placing the flowers, as I was able to hang each as you would hang ornaments on a Christmas tree. This jubilant design creates a vibrant frame for a guest of honor or celebrating couple—a perfect focal point for all the celebrations that life brings.

TIPS:

- Bittersweet and porcelain vine are invasive plants in some areas. If you use these, or any plants identified as invasive or noxious in your region, be sure to collect and dispose of them responsibly. I use a tarp when harvesting anything seed-rich and potentially harmful—such as wild grape, porcelain vine, bittersweet, elaeagnus, or knotweed—to prevent spreading seeds, and I compost these with my municipal compost to ensure that the seeds are destroyed as the plant material is processed.

- Lisianthus appear delicate and papery but are actually quite sturdy and long-lasting. I designed this arch a day before, and I sprayed the hanging lisianthus with water to give it a little boost. Flowers displayed upside down have gravity on their side, so they're less prone to wilting.

WALL FLOWERS

I've always loved marigolds. Their spicy scent, vibrant colors, and ruffled, strokable heads are irresistible. I grow a small patch of them every year, and whenever I see them at the market I just have to snatch them up. When I came across farmer Caitlin Mathes's Instagram account and learned that she loves these flowers so much she made the choice to grow them exclusively, I was really tickled. Her charming single-crop farm, the Marigold Gardens, currently grows more than fifty varieties in all colors of the sunset, from soft lemon yellow to deep rust. Caitlin sells these as cut flowers, but it's her beautiful garlands that really caught my eye. Native to Mexico and Guatemala, marigolds have traveled the world, becoming an important flower used in celebrations, rituals, and ceremonies for hundreds of years, often in garland form. Inspired to string some up and make something punchy and celebratory to show my love for these bright beauties, I reached out to Caitlin, who sent me hundreds of blooms by mail. I strung them by variety and hung them alongside foraged ash seed clusters and hanging amaranth. To capture the celebratory feel of this composition, I threw a handful of marigold and aster petal confetti into the air just as as this piece was photographed.

TIPS:

- To make the structure for this floral wall hanging, I hung several 12-inch [30.5 cm] chicken wire burritos from a sturdy steel rod. The burritos hung down from the rod like pendants, disappearing as the ash seed clusters and amaranths were tucked into their numerous nooks and crannies. I hung some of the shorter marigold strands from the rod, allowing one end to hang free. I hung the longer garlands like swags, attaching both ends to the rod. I really liked the interplay between the naturally cascading forms and the handcrafted garlands. See the section on Chicken Wire Forms (page 30) for more on using chicken wire to create reliable inner workings for floral compositions.

- The vibrant mix of colors made this a very energetic composition, but these materials also dry beautifully, fading into a mix of subtle earth tones. Consider creating a piece for a short-term celebration like a wedding or festival, then allowing it to dry naturally and live on as natural wall art.

AERIAL AMARYLLIS

The most effortless way to create an impressive, memorable floral display is to attach natural materials to an interesting structural or architectural element in a space. The hanging pendant chandelier in this composition provided the perfect foundation for this interesting selection of golden holly berry, lacy dried knotweed, and peach amaryllis. The fixture provided many secure attachment points, allowing me to easily embellish it. Simple twists of bind wire transformed a lovely light fixture into a celebratory aerial floral display. The petite peach Oh Flora compote vases (see Resources, page 171) held additional amaryllis, filling out the design. Consider creating a hanging floral display for an extra-special in-home celebration such as a New Year's Eve dinner with friends.

TIP:

- Amaryllis aren't commonly thought of as a cut flower, but they are incredibly long-lasting, versatile, and impactful. Their hollow, straw-like stems lend themselves well to hanging installations. To use them this way, fill the hollow stem with dampened cotton or even plain water, to keep the flowers hydrated while they're displayed. Then use stem wrap tape to fortify the end of the stem and prevent it from curling. Insert a wire through this taped area and bend it into a hook.

FLOWER TOWER

An inexpensive steel grounding rod from the hardware store and an everyday patio umbrella stand combine to create a sturdy backbone for this artful sculpture. A tube of chicken wire adds body to the skeleton, allowing me to display show-stopping 'River City' heirloom mums from Harmony Harvest Farm, late-season marigolds, coral winterberries, and dried hops vine from my garden. The flowers are incredible, but the stars of this composition might be the gooseneck gourds—purchased dried, preserved, and ready to use from an Amish farm. I love their wacky forms and reddish-blond color. They remind me of fantastical brass instruments waiting to be played. Create an art piece like this for a celebration or as an impressive natural sculpture to display in the home.

TIPS:

- To create the skeleton for this tower, insert a grounding rod into a stand base and tighten it until it's solidly locked in place. Create a long, tubular chicken wire burrito (see page 23 for more) long enough to span the entire length of the rod. Fold the very end of the chicken wire tube over the top of the rod and secure it to the rod with bind wire before wrapping the rest of the length loosely around the rod. Secure the other end of the chicken wire tube at the base of the rod with more bind wire. Choose three areas to concentrate the gourds: one high, one central, and one at the base. Attach the gourds to the rod by wiring them to the chicken wire and to each other. After the gourds have been distributed, arrange the ilex berries, mums, and marigolds

in the empty pockets of chicken wire. Finish the design by tucking in delicate tendrils of hops vine.

- Treat fresh flowers in the hydration chamber to prepare them for a short-term display such as this. To create a permanent sculpture, replace the fresh flowers with dried blooms, grasses, pods, or berries. See Simple Design Mechanics and Techniques (page 29) for more.

RELIABLES

*KEY

⌒ Good for use in wearables

⊲⊳ Strong stem, good for use in large-scale installs

🖋 Vulnerable stem, good for use in installs with internal support (wire, wooden skewer) or external structural support

FOLIAGE

acacia (knifeblade, pearl, feather) ⌒ ⊲⊳

acuba ⌒ ⊲⊳

agonis ⌒ ⊲⊳

aralia ⌒ ⊲⊳

baker fern/leather leaf ⌒ ⊲⊳

bay laurel ⌒ ⊲⊳

Berzelia ⌒ ⊲⊳

bittersweet (late season) ⌒ ⊲⊳

blueberry branch ⌒ ⊲⊳

boxwood ⌒ ⊲⊳

brake fern ⌒ ⊲⊳

brunia ⌒ ⊲⊳

calathea ⌒ ⊲⊳

callicarpa ⌒ ⊲⊳

camellia ⌒ ⊲⊳

chinaberry ⌒ 🖋

coral fern ⌒ ⊲⊳

datura pod ⌒ ⊲⊳

dracaena ⌒ ⊲⊳

dracaena 'Song of India' ⌒ ⊲⊳

elaeagnus, all varieties ⌒ ⊲⊳

eucalyptus, all varieties ⌒ ⊲⊳

euonymus ⌒ ⊲⊳

evergreens, all ⌒ ⊲⊳

fig on the branch ⌒ ⊲⊳

flax ⌒ ⊲⊳

Galax urceolata ⌒ ⊲⊳

grasses ⌒ ⊲⊳

grevillea ⌒ ⊲⊳

Hakea laurina ⌒ ⊲⊳

hala (Pandanus tectorius) ⌒ ⊲⊳

holly ⌒ ⊲⊳

honey myrtle

huckleberry

ilex

ivy (common, vine type)

ivy (hedera, bush type)

kakuma fern

kochia

kumquat on the branch

leucadendron

lipstick pods

lotus pods

Lycopodium

magnolia

maranta

Ming fern (*Asparagus macowanii*)

monstera

mulberry

myrtle

Nageia nagi (Asian bayberry)

nandina

oak

olive branch

oregonia (variegated boxwood)

palm

pear (ornamental)

penny cress

pepperberry

persimmon on the branch

Photinia

Pieris japonica

pineapple

pittosporum, all varieties

plumosus fern

Podocarpus

pomegranate on the branch

poppy pods

privet

pyracantha

raspberry (ornamental)

rose sumac

rosemary

Ruscus asculeatus (butcher's broom), all varieties

salal/lemon leaf 🎩 🏋

skimmia 🎩 🌾

smilax, bagged 🎩 🏋

smilax, southern 🎩 🌾

snowberry 🎩 🏋

succulents 🎩 🌾

ti leaves 🎩 🌾

tillandsia 🎩 🏋

tree-of-heaven (*Ailanthus altissima*) seedpods 🎩 🏋

tropicals, most 🎩 🏋

Viburnum tinus 🎩 🏋

woolly bush (*Adenanthos sericeus*) 🎩 🏋

FLOWERS

Some have soft or fleshy stems that may sag with time, but the blooms will hold well. Take this into consideration, and choose your placements accordingly. Allow cascading blooms to cascade naturally instead of forcing them upward. Insert stems in a direction that will allow them to look their best for the length of the event. Large fleshy stems such as hyacinth and amaryllis can be bolstered by inserting a slim bamboo skewer.

agapanthus 🎩 🏋

ageratum 🎩 🌾

allium, all varieties 🎩 🌾

Alstroemeria (Peruvian lily) 🎩 🌾

amaranthus, upright 🎩 🏋

amaryllis 🎩 🌾

anthurium 🎩 🏋

artichoke 🎩 🏋

Asiatic lily 🎩 🏋

banana flower 🎩 🏋

banksia 🎩 🏋

begonia 🎩 🌾

Berzelia 🎩 🏋

Boronia 🎩 🏋

bouvardia (limited testing) 🎩 🏋

bromeliad 🎩 🏋

calathea 🎩 🏋

calla lily 🎩 🏋

calycina 🎩 🏋

carnation 🎩 🌾

celosia, cockscomb 🎩 🏋

chamomile, button 🎩 🏋

chrysanthemum (the firm, plump varieties) 🥣 🏋

craspedia 🥣 🏋

crocosmia 🥣 🏋

curcuma 👒 🏋

cypripedium (lady's slipper) 🥣 🏋

dahlia (firm ball type, locally sourced) 👒 🌾

date palm 🥣 🏋

dianthus 'Green Trick' 🥣 🏋

dianthus (sweet William) 👒 🏋

echinacea 🥣 🏋

echinops 👒 🏋

eremurus 👒 🏋

Eriostemon 👒 🏋

eryngium 🥣 🏋

eucomis 🥣 🏋

festival bush 🥣 🏋

forsythia 🥣 🏋

freesia 👒 🏋

Fritillaria imperialis 🥣 🌾

Fritillaria persica

garden rose (firm, South American, especially Juliet and Campanella) 🥣 🏋

Genista 🥣 🏋

gerrondo gerbera daisy 🥣 🌾

ginger (beehive, wax, torch, shell, shampoo) 🥣 🏋

gladiola 🥣 🏋

gloriosa 🥣 🏋

grevillia 🥣 🏋

gypsophila 🥣 🏋

heather 🥣 🏋

heliconia, all varieties 🥣 🏋

Heliconia psittacorum 🥣 🏋

hellebore (mature, after seed head forms) 🥣 🌾

hyacinth 🥣 🌾

hybrid tea rose 🥣 🏋

hydrangea (late season antique) 🥣 🏋

hypericum 🥣 🏋

ixia 🥣 🏋

kalanchoe 🥣 🏋

kangaroo paw 👒 🏋

leptospermum

liatris

limonium

lipstick pods

lisianthus, doubles

marigold

martigon lily

nerine lily

orchids (cymbidium, dendro-
bium, mokara, oncidium, vanda)

Ornithogalum arabicum, *Ornithogalum dubium*, and *Ornithogalum thyrsoides*

Pieris japonica

pompon mums

protea, all varieties

rice flower

rose sumac

safflower

Sandersonia aurantiaca

Serruria

skimmia, blooming

squill

statice

Sterling Range (*Ciliatum*)

Stirlingia

Strelitzia (bird of paradise)

tanacetum, tansy

tuberose

tulip, doubles

Verticordia

Waratah

waxflower

yarrow

RESOURCES

FLOWERS, FOLIAGE, AND OTHER MATERIALS

ARGUS FARM STOP
www.argusfarmstop.com
Year-round daily farmers' market supplying the community with produce and flowers provided by more than two hundred local growers.

Based in Ann Arbor, Michigan.

DUTCH FLOWER LINE
www.dutchflowerline.com
Incredible selection of the finest quality cut flowers.

Based in New York City; flowers shipped throughout the United States.

GRATEFUL GARDENERS
www.gratefulgardeners.co
Organic and inventive flower farm that offers an expansive array of premium quality blooms.

Based in Montgomery County, Maryland.

GRAYE'S GREENHOUSE
www.grayesgreenhouse.com
Destination greenhouse providing hundreds of unique plants, vegetable starts, pollinator favorites, and perennials, including native species.

Based in Plymouth, Michigan.

HARMONY HARVEST FARM
www.hhfshop.com
Wonderful, wide selection of farm-fresh flowers, foliage, heirloom plants, dried materials, and more!

Based in Virginia; flowers shipped throughout the United States.

LOCAL HARVEST
www.localharvest.org
Resource for finding local farms throughout the United States.

LUELLA ACRES
www.luellaacres.com
Source for premium, unique seasonal blooms.

Based in Dexter, Michigan.

THE MARIGOLD GARDENS
www.themarigoldgardens.com
Incredible flower farm where self-proclaimed "marigold monger" and artist Caitlin Mathes grows more than forty varieties.

Based in Ithaca, New York.

MARILLA FIELD & FLORA
www.marillafield.com
Exquisite farm-fresh flowers and foliage, grown by Adrianne Gammie, a farmer with a florist's eye!

Based in Dexter, Michigan.

MAYESH WHOLESALE FLORIST
www.mayesh.com
Wonderful resource for professional florists. Large selection of US-grown flowers and foliage.

Multiple locations; flowers and supplies shipped throughout the United States.

MICHIGAN FLOWER GROWERS COOPERATIVE
www.miflowercoop.com
Cooperative offering a wide selection of locally grown flowers and foliage in an aggregated weekly marketplace.

Based in Ypsilanti, Michigan.

SEELEY FARM
www.seeleyfarm.com
Fantastic farm offering a wonderful selection of vegetables, cut flowers, and plants.

Based in Ann Arbor, Michigan.

SLOW FARM
www.slowfarmandfriends.com
Certified organic U-pick farm and farmstand devoted to the principles of Slow Food, agroecology, and justice in the food system.

Based in Ann Arbor, Michigan.

SLOW FLOWERS
www.slowflowers.com
Online directory of sources for cut flowers throughout the United States that serves to connect flower lovers with local flower growers.

Based outside of Ann Arbor, Michigan.

WHIPSTONE FARM
www.whipstone.com
Family farm growing the highest-quality, naturally grown cut flowers, produce, and edible flowers.

Based in Prescott, Arizona.

VESSELS, MECHANICS, AND OTHER SUPPLIES

AMISH GOURDS
www.amishgourds.com
Cooperative venture sourcing dried crafting gourds from numerous Pennsylvania Dutch Amish farm families and shipping them to gourd lovers throughout the United States.

ARTIFACT UPRISING
www.artifactuprising.com
Online resource for turning digital images into high-quality prints.

AVERY WILLIAMSON
www.averywilliamson.com
Multidisciplinary artist whose work in weaving, photography, and drawing explores the narratives of Black women in personal and institutional archives. Avery's expressive, functional art cubes inspired many of the designs in this book.

BENJAMIN MAIER CERAMICS
www.maierceramics.com
Functional and artful pottery created in Leland, Michigan.

BLACK WING CLAY
@blackwingclay
Talented ceramicist duo creating incredible functional art for restaurants, florists, and art lovers in San Francisco, California.

FLORAL GENIUS
www.floralgenius.com
Only US manufacturer of pin and cup-style flower holders and the world's only maker of Blue Ribbon hairpin flower holders.

MAY ARTS
www.mayarts.com
Wholesale ribbon supplier, offering a wide selection of high-quality silk ribbons at an affordable price.

NOE KUREMOTO
www.noekuremoto.com
Exquisite, emotive, hand-crafted vessels created in London by ceramic artist Noe Kuremoto.

OH FLORA STORE
www.ohflorastore.com
Beautiful, ethically made small-batch ceramics designed by an event florist for flower lovers everywhere.

POTTERY BARN
www.potterybarn.com
Stylish tableware, vessels, and home decor at accessible prices.

RAAWII
www.raawii.eu
Passionate, design-driven company that creates modern, functional art products for the home. Based in Copenhagen.

RINGS & THINGS
www.rings-things.com
Source for jewelry-making supplies and tools.

SAVE-ON-CRAFTS
www.save-on-crafts.com
Hobbyist's resource for floral and crafting supplies.

SYNDICATE SALES
www.syndicatesales.com
Supply resource for clear water tubes, florist-grade chicken wire, straight and paddle wire, and Holly Chapple bud vases and footed bowls.

TARA DOUGLASS CERAMICS
www.brooklynplantstudio.com
Expressive, artful ceramic vessels created by a florist for flower lovers.

TARGET
www.target.com
Source for fashionable, affordable flat-ware, glassware, and tableware.

FURTHER LEARNING

THE ART OF WEARABLE FLOWERS BY SUSAN MCLEARY
Learn how to make more than forty floral wearables with this step-by-step guide.

ASSOCIATION OF SPECIALTY CUT FLOWER GROWERS
www.ascfg.org
Nonprofit trade association for commercial cut flower growers that educates and unites growers, designers, suppliers, buyers, and researchers.

PASSIONFLOWER SUE
www.passionflowersue.com
Hub for online classes focusing on artful, forward-thinking floral design.

ACKNOWLEDGMENTS

This book is for the flower people. Not just flower-obsessed florists like me, but for all who feel even vaguely drawn to or inspired by flowers. I hope the ideas within feel welcoming, accessible, and inspiring. I hope this book invites new flower people to bring flowers home more often and engage with them in a more meaningful way. I hope it encourages seasoned flower people to pause more often to create for their own enjoyment.

First, a thank you to my mother, master gardener Elizabeth McLeary, for the artful, inspiring home environment and extraordinary gardens I grew up with. I know that I was lucky to be exposed to the wonders of flowers right from the start. Our home was always filled with plants, and extensive, flower-filled gardens erupted from every available outdoor space. She created an incredible amount of beauty with just her tenacity and bare hands. I witnessed her efforts and saw how much she relished the natural spaces she tended. I'm certain this example has much to do with my passion for flowers and how I choose to share this passion with the world.

This book is also a love letter to the flower people that make it possible for us to hold magic in our hands. The growers, large and small; the flower sellers, near and far; and the shops, studios, home gardeners, and designers that see the value in offering beauty in flower form to others.

Heartfelt thanks to the people responsible for the beautiful flowers in this book. My local sources: Argus Farm Stop, Graye's Greenhouse, Luella Acres, Marilla Field & Flora, the Michigan Flower Growers' Cooperative, Seeley Farm, Slow Farm, and the Ann Arbor Farmer's Market. Even though our growing season is short (zone 5), these dedicated growers and markets lovingly provide a wonderful and plentiful supply of interesting plants and flowers over as much of the year as possible. I look forward to the treasures I'll find from them at the start of each season.

Thanks also to the growers and sellers that make it possible for me to enjoy incredible flowers beyond Michigan. I was thrilled to work with materials from Mayesh, the Marigold Gardens, Whipstone Farm, Harmony Harvest, Dutch Flower Line, Amish Gourds, and Grateful Gardeners. It is always so exciting to receive a delivery from these dedicated people, and it was truly a pleasure to design with these materials.

Thank you to my friend, Slow Flowers visionary Debra Prinzing. I met her early in my floral journey, and she inspired me to see flowers in a more holistic way. The Slow Flowers movement caused a real awareness shift in me and has strengthened my purpose and enriched my work. It was meaningful for me to work within season, instead of simply filling these pages with all my favorite things. This focus on seasonality and locality increases our appreciation for the exact place on earth we call home and strengthens our communities by supporting local agriculture and sustainable practices.

Thank you to the photographer for this book, Emily Berger. I've been a fan of her stunning food photography for years, so it was a thrill to collaborate with her. Her patience, creativity, keen eye, and calm manner made the work feel effortless. She is also a gifted gardener, so it felt right and good to work with her on this project.

Many thanks to Chronicle Books and my editor Rachel Hiles for taking interest in my point of view and giving me the opportunity to offer a second book to the field I love. I am a person who works in ephemera, so it's incredibly gratifying to be able to contribute in this tangible, lasting way.

Thank you to my agents, Leslie Jonath and Leslie Stoker, for their insight, encouragement, and knowledge. Thank you for helping me once again navigate the unfamiliar waters of book making!

Thank you to the artists who created the incredible vessels that enliven my home. A special thank you to ceramicist Noe Kuremoto. Her work informed many of my design choices in this book. Her vessels are so special—sculptural, textural, and full of personality. The collection of vessels I have from her hands have become treasured members of my family!

Thank you to LaPorcshia Winfield, Issac Coenca, Chauné Rael-Whitsitt, and Naomi Ning, who appear in this book and have brought my work to life. A special thank you to principal model, Chauné, who is as kind and thoughtful as she is beautiful. It's been such a pleasure to work with you over the years! A warm thank you to makeup artist Esther Soto, whose expert hand and gentle manner make all people touched by her brushes feel wonderful. Your enthusiasm and talent will take you far.